Artificial Intelligence and Quantum Computing
Next-Generation Technologies

Table of Contents

Chapter 1. Introduction

In this Special Report, we will explore the ever-evolving realms of Artificial Intelligence and Quantum Computing - two next-generation technologies set to redefine our modern landscape. This might sound technical and perhaps intimidating, but don't go away just yet! We've designed this report in an approachable manner, uniquely bridging the gap between the complex world of advanced technologies and day-to-day lives. If you've ever been curious about AI's potential scope or mystified by what Quantum Computing is all about, this report is your friendly guide to understanding these revolutionary spheres. So, whether you're a tech enthusiast, a business leader, or a curious learner, take this leap into the future - one page at a time.

Chapter 2. Exploring the Essence of Artificial Intelligence

Artificial Intelligence, often simply referred to as AI, can seem like a sophisticated and intimidating concept. However, it is increasingly becoming essential to our daily lives. With the guidance of machine learning and algorithms, AI is shaping industries, transforming economies, and influencing how we interact with technology.

2.1. Understanding AI

At its core, Artificial Intelligence is a branch of computer science that involves creating systems or machines capable of tasks that require human intelligence, such as understanding natural language, recognizing patterns, solving problems, and making decisions.

AI systems can vary in complexity, from relatively simple rules-based engines to sophisticated models based on neural networks that can "learn" from data.

2.2. The History of AI

AI is often perceived as a new technology, yet the concept has been around for decades. In 1950, British mathematician and cryptanalyst Alan Turing proposed the "Turing Test" as a measure of the ability of a machine to demonstrate human-like intelligence. His work is often credited as the foundation of artificial intelligence.

It was in 1956 that the term "Artificial Intelligence" was coined at a Dartmouth College conference, indicating the birth of AI as a defined field. The journey since then, however, has been characterized by periods of optimism and disillusionment, known as AI winters, when the widespread hope around AI's potential gives way to disappointment with slow progress.

However, the explosion of data and advances in computational power in the 21st century have brought AI back to the fore with renewed vigor, further triggering wide-ranging implications across industries and society.

2.3. Categories of AI

AI generally falls into two categories: Narrow AI, which is an AI system designed to perform a narrow task (e.g., facial recognition or internet searches), and General AI, which refers to systems or machines that could successfully perform any intellectual task that a human being can.

While we're still in the early stages of achieving General AI, Narrow AI is becoming quite common, embedded in many of the applications we use on a daily basis.

2.4. Machine Learning and Deep Learning

When talking about AI, it is impossible not to mention Machine Learning (ML) and Deep Learning. Often used interchangeably with AI, they are a subset of it.

Machine learning is a method of data analysis that automates analytical model building. Using algorithms that iteratively learn from data, machine learning allows computers to find hidden insights without being explicitly programmed where to look.

Deep learning, on the other hand, is a technique for implementing machine learning. It uses a multi-layered structure of algorithms called neural networks, designed to mimic the way a human brain works, and can learn and make intelligent decisions on its own.

Together, they power advanced AI functionality, such as image and speech recognition, recommendation systems, and autonomous vehicles.

2.5. The Real-life Impact of AI

Artificial Intelligence is notably transforming many segments of the economy and society at large, providing solutions in healthcare, climate modeling, financial services, transportation, agriculture, among other fields.

Thanks to AI, doctors can diagnose diseases more accurately, farmers can monitor crop yields more efficiently, and businesses can predict customer behavior accurately.

However, AI also presents ethical conundrums, particularly in areas like data privacy and job displacement. Balancing AI's benefits against its potential disadvantages call for continued debate and prudent policies.

2.6. The Future of AI

In the future, AI is expected to continue advancing exponentially and gradually. As AI continues to mature, it must work in harmony with human intelligence to drive innovation, efficiency, and productivity.

While fully autonomous AI is still a thing for distant future, the increasingly sophisticated AI models have started making their presence felt. Improved natural language generation and understanding, more efficient learning systems, and progress in AI safety are among the emerging trends shaping the future of AI.

As we take strides towards a more AI-driven world, it's imperative that we understand and engage with this transformative technology, rather than fearing it. While challenges abound, the potential rewards of AI – a seamless blend of man and machine working in concert – are manifold and hold the promise of an exciting future.

Chapter 3. Quantum Computing: Decoding the Basics

Quantum Computing is a rapidly expanding field, but to appreciate it, we first need to explore the fundamental principles that underpin this discipline.

3.1. The Quantum World

Quantum physics, the science at the heart of quantum computing, is nothing short of awe-inspiring. It's fundamentally different from classical physics, contrasting the world of waves, particles and uncertainty with the expected determinacy of macroscopic phenomena.

At its core, Quantum physics consists of atoms, molecules, electrons or even light broken down into its most basic units. In these minute realms, distinct and peculiar rules apply. Particles can exist in multiple states simultaneously and can deeply influence one another, irrespective of the distances separating them. These phenomena are respectively called superposition and entanglement.

This is where quantum computing extends beyond classical computing. Classical bits are binary, taking on a definitive state of either 0 or 1. Quantum bits, or "qubits", vastly differ. A qubit can be both 0 and 1 at the same time, courtesy of superposition. This mysterious state ends when the qubit is observed, forcing it to collapse to either 0 or 1.

3.2. Hardware and the Qubit

The heart of quantum computers is their use of qubits instead of traditional bits. As mentioned, a qubit can exist in a superposition of states, meaning it can represent 0, 1, or both states simultaneously. It's this property that allows quantum computers to compute faster and solve problems inaccessible to classical machines.

But how are these qubits built? Various physical systems can serve as qubits. Scientists use superconducting circuits, trapped ions, topological qubits, or even neutral atoms to harness quantum properties. Each approach has its advantages and challenges, such as creating a stable environment, error correction, and scalability - issues that must be addressed for quantum computing to become a practical technology.

3.3. Quantum Gates and Circuits

The foundation of any computation, whether classical or quantum, are logical operations. In classical computing, these are performed by gates, such as AND, OR, and NOT gates. Quantum computing, true to its nature, employs quantum gates, which create transformations across the states within quantum systems.

These transformations are complex, using probabilities and even allowing for reversible computation, unlike their classical counterparts. Common quantum gates include the Pauli-X, Pauli-Y, Pauli-Z, and the Hadamard gate. By stringing together these gates, quantum circuits are formed, which in turn can compute unique and complex calculations.

An important perspective to remember is that these operations are not just transformation but also manipulations in a high-dimensional space. This multidimensionality distinguishes quantum computing from classical computing, setting the stage for solving complex problems.

3.4. Quantum Algorithms

Quantum algorithms incorporate these logical quantum gate operations to solve a problem. A notable algorithm is Shor's algorithm for integer factorization, which has implications in cryptography and is more efficient than classical algorithms.

Grover's algorithm, another important quantum algorithm, offers quadratically faster searches through unstructured databases. This can revolutionize database searching, optimization problems, and solving systems of linear equations.

As quantum computing matures, more algorithms will likely surface, each taking advantage of different aspects of quantum systems, and potentially reshaping computational tasks as we know them.

3.5. Quantum Computing's Challenges & Future

Despite its extraordinary potential, quantum computing faces significant hurdles. Aside from technical challenges like creating stable qubits and achieving error correction, there's a high barrier to entry in understanding and applying quantum principles.

Standard breakthroughs are needed to mature quantum hardware. Quantum computers work in incredibly delicate conditions, making them prone to 'quantum noise'. Minimizing such noise, which causes errors in calculations, is another major issue currently being tackled.

The future of quantum computing remains promising. While we're still in the early stages, research into addressing these challenges is underway. Once they are overcome, we could potentially see quantum computing revolutionize fields such as cryptography, material science, drug discovery, and more.

But without a doubt, understanding and leveraging quantum computing requires a mindset that embraces not just the distinct science it represents, but also the transformative potential it holds. This journey of quantum discovery might challenge our intellects, but it won't be short of extraordinary revelations, guaranteed to reshape our perception of reality and technology. In the grandest scheme, that's perhaps a tiny price to pay!

Chapter 4. Interplay Between AI and Quantum Computing

While Artificial Intelligence (AI) and Quantum Computing may be independent entities, they are like two sides of the same coin. Each greatly impacts the power and potential of the other. This 'interplay' evolves every day, creating a synergy that continually propels technology forward.

4.1. From Bits to Qubits

Traditional computing operates using binary "bits", either a 0 or a 1. It's like a light switch that's either on or off. Quantum Computing takes it a level up by using "qubits". A qubit could be both 0 and 1 simultaneously, thanks to a principle called superposition. This simultaneousness leads to enormous potential for computational power, exponentially increasing with every added qubit.

An appropriate analogy would be reading a book. While a traditional computer would read the book page by page, a quantum computer could read all the pages simultaneously due to superposition, thus greatly enhancing the speed.

4.2. Quantum Boost for AI

The first transformative impact of this interplay comes from the acceleration that Quantum Computing can offer AI. Machine Learning models, a core component of AI, typically require vast amounts of data processing and pattern recognition. Traditional computational systems may take days, weeks, or even months, depending on the complexity of the task and the data set's size.

Quantum computers, with their ability to process information simultaneously, could drastically cut down this time, enabling AI to learn faster and on a much grander scale. Quantum algorithms like Quantum Support Vector Machine (QSVM) and Quantum Principal Component Analysis (QPCA) have shown potential in speeding up tasks like classification and regression in machine learning.

4.3. Quantum Inspired AI

The next dimension to explore is not just about Quantum Computing enhancing AI, but AI learning from Quantum phenomena. Scientists now look towards quantum mechanics to improve artificial neurons, the building blocks of Machine Learning. Much like the superposition principle in Quantum Computing, the neurons could hold numerous states simultaneously, increasing informational capacity.

This concept forms the basis of "Quantum Machine Learning" or QML. It blends quantum algorithms with machine learning methods, promising to resolve complex problems, especially ones involving unstructured data which conventional AI struggles to manage.

4.4. Quantum-proof AI

With power comes the need for protection. Quantum Computing, while bringing numerous benefits, also poses a risk in terms of cybersecurity. Today's encryption systems, often used in AI implementations, rely on the complexity of factoring large numbers— a task that's hard for classical computers but straightforward for quantum ones.

AI will have to evolve to be "quantum-proof" to ensure continued security in the age of Quantum Computing. There's growing buzz around quantum cryptography and post-quantum cryptography in AI ecosystems to counteract the decryption power of Quantum Computing.

4.5. Future by Intersection: Quantum AI

We're looking at a future where AI and Quantum Computing don't just co-exist, but intricately intertwine to birth Quantum AI. Quantum AI refers to using quantum computing for computation of machine learning algorithms. Experiments conducted by Alphabet's X, the company's moonshot factory, have shown that Quantum AI could be viable and incredibly powerful, heralding the next stage of machine intelligence.

Quantum AI uses specific quantum algorithms, like Quantum Approximate Optimization Algorithm (QAOA) and Variational Quantum Eigensolver (VQE), to solve complex optimization and cognitive tasks.

4.6. Challenges and Controversies

As promising as Quantum AI sounds, there are substantial challenges before it becomes a reality. Quantum systems are expensive, difficult to maintain, and scale. They also require a near absolute zero temperature to function, making them less practical. Apart from technical challenges, there are philosophical and ethical debates to consider.

In a nutshell, the interplay between AI and Quantum Computing, forms a perfect symbiosis that has the power to revolutionize various sectors – from healthcare to finance, climate science to cybersecurity, and more.

There is power in this synergy, and as we continue to explore the ramifications, we realize that we are only scratching the surface of what the future could look like. There's a long journey ahead, but each step promises to be exciting, transformative, and empowering towards an advanced, inclusive, and sustainable world.

Chapter 5. The Role of AI in Today's Digital Age

Artificial Intelligence (AI) is predominantly reshaping every aspect of our lives with each passing day. It is one of the finest creations by human minds—aptly referred to as the 'crowning achievement of human intellect'.

5.1. Understanding the Basics

To appreciate the role of AI in today's digital age, let's first understand the basics. AI is a multidisciplinary domain of computer science that simulates human intelligence in machines. The products designed along these lines tend to learn, reason, and self-correct. AI is broadly categorized into two types: narrow (or weak) AI and general (or strong) AI. The former is exclusively trained for specific tasks, such as voice recognition, while the latter is an advanced form of AI, possessing the cognitive abilities similar to humans.

The discipline of AI encompasses diverse fields, including robotics, natural language processing, voice recognition, heuristic classification, neural networks, and much more. Each of these fields employs AI principles to create intelligent systems capable of performing tasks with minimal human intervention.

5.2. The Evolution of AI

The journey of AI evolution is an interesting one; from a mere concept in computer literature to one of the prime influencers of technology in the 21st century. AI research started post World War II when a group of visionary computer scientists believed mechanisms could be developed that mimic human brain behaviour. Over time, AI has evolved dramatically, absorbing new techniques and advances from many related disciplines.

The defining period in the evolution of AI was the availability of big data and radical growth in computational capabilities. With these developments, AI's maturation journey became steeper, and with machine learning and deep learning techniques, the AI industry saw a revolution like never before. Today, the integration of AI can be observed in almost all facets of modern life.

5.3. AI: The Game Changer

AI has begun to impact industries, economies, and our daily lives profoundly. Not only does it provide the tools for businesses to streamline operations, but also opens explorative doors to new innovations and opportunities. It acts as a catalyst for social development and has tremendous potential to foster economic growth.

In healthcare, for instance, AI is revolutionizing diagnostic methodologies and enhancing patient care. Automated image diagnosis, predictive analytics, virtual healthcare support, and precise surgery are just some manifestations of AI in healthcare.

The transportation industry is seeing a dramatic transformation with AI-powered self-driving cars and intelligent traffic management systems. E-commerce, entertainment, and education sectors are similarly reaping the benefits of AI, providing personalized experiences and smarter services.

AI is also improving the proficiency of decision-making processes by offering predictive and prescriptive tools. Its capabilities are perfect for sectors such as finance, where numerous variables need analysis for effective decision-making.

5.4. AI and Economic Development

One of the hottest topics of current interest involves examining AI's influence on global economic development. Studies suggest that AI could double the annual economic growth rates by 2035 by changing the nature of work and forming a new relationship between man and machine.

AI can boost labor productivity by up to 40% by enabling people to use their time more efficiently. Moreover, AI could also serve as an enabler in solving complex social challenges. By enabling more efficient, insightful, and inclusive public services, AI holds the potential to create incredible social value.

AI might also cause displacement of certain jobs that could be automated. However, it is also gearing towards creating new types of jobs, demanding new skillsets. Thus, it becomes necessary to prepare the current and future workforce to effectively participate in an AI-driven economy.

5.5. Challenges Ahead

Despite the vast potential and accomplishments, AI is not without its share of challenges. Issues concerning privacy, security, ethical concerns, data management, accountability, and job displacement are critical.

For AI to be beneficial, it must be used responsibly, keeping ethical guidelines and societal implications in mind. As policymakers, we need to identify strategies that leverage AI's benefits while mitigating its potential harm.

Challenges for AI also lie in overcoming technical limitations. Though AI exhibits intelligent behavior, it lacks an understanding of contexts. There is still much to be done in areas such as advanced reasoning, common-sense understanding, and autonomous learning.

5.6. The Road Ahead

Looking ahead, AI has the potential to become the most transformative technology of the 21st century. It is at the forefront of technology driving digital transformations across sectors.

The future points towards more sophisticated AI systems, capable of self-learning, reasoning, and problem-solving. As we dream of a world with friendly robots and AI everywhere, continued dynamic advancements in technology, research, and infrastructure promise to make these dreams a reality.

AI is hence, a remarkable journey, a story of human triumph—continuously reaching for the stars, challenging the norm, and pushing the boundaries of technological breakthroughs. This is the dawn of the AI era!

Much like the invention of wheel or electricity has brought significant changes in human history, AI unfolds a new chapter in the digital age. We are walking into an era where AI will not only augment human productivity but also build partnership between humans and machines that complement each other's strengths. Whether it's about predicting trends in stock markets or detecting life-threatening diseases, AI has emerged as the game-changer, heralding an era of immense technological revolution.

Chapter 6. Quantum Computing: Boundaries and Possibilities

Let's embark on an immersive journey into the fascinating world of quantum computing, its boundaries, and the limitless possibilities it presents.

6.1. Defining Quantum Computing

Quantum Computing is a sizable leap from traditional computing. At its core, it is an emerging technology that harnesses the principles of quantum mechanics — a branch of physics that explores the behavior of particles at the atomic and subatomic levels. Traditional computing relies on bits, binary units that carry either a 0 or a 1. In stark contrast, quantum computing deploys quantum bits, often referred to as qubits, which can be both a 0 and a 1 at the same time, courtesy of a property called superposition.

Superposition lies at the heart of the quantum computer's power and potential. This enables quantum computers to process an exponentially larger set of possibilities compared to classical computers. Their unique ability to handle multiple states concurrently opens the door to solving complex computational problems at speeds that were previously unimaginable.

6.2. Quantum Entanglement: A Deep Dive

The underlying principle of quantum computing is quantum entanglement. This phenomenon of quantum mechanics is so strange that even Albert Einstein was compelled to call it "spooky action at a distance". In simple terms, entanglement establishes a connection between particles so that the state of one particle instantly corresponds with the state of another, no matter the distance.

In the context of quantum computing, quantum entanglement allows qubits that are entangled to communicate information more efficiently than classical bits. The entangled qubits work together in a way that makes computations faster and more efficient, which is pivotal for tackling complex or large-scale computational tasks.

6.3. Quantum Supremacy: Breaking New Ground

The term 'quantum supremacy' relates to the point where a quantum computer can perform tasks that are practically impossible for a classical computer to solve within a reasonable timeframe. In 2019, tech giant Google claimed to have achieved quantum supremacy with its 54-qubit processor, Sycamore. They announced that this processor solved a specific problem in 200 seconds that would take the world's most powerful supercomputer 10,000 years.

While these claims have sparked debate within the scientific community, they certainly put into perspective the potential of quantum computers for unprecedented computing speeds. However, achieving true and universal quantum supremacy — where quantum computers outperform classical ones at all tasks — still has many technical challenges and barriers to overcome.

6.4. Limitations of Quantum Computing

Despite its promising prospect, quantum computing faces several limitations that are worth acknowledging:

- **Coherence**: Quantum states are delicate and can easily be disturbed or 'decohered'. Maintaining the overall coherence of qubits for a reasonable duration is a significant challenge.

- **Error Correction**: Quantum computing is highly susceptible to errors. A tiny disturbance can cause a qubit to flip state, leading to an error in computation. Developing efficient quantum error correction techniques remains a critical aspect of quantum computing research.

- **Scalability**: Building practical quantum computers requires controlling a large array of qubits. However, ensuring the reliable and robust operation of such systems is difficult, making scalability a notable concern.

6.5. Applications and Possibilities

While there are challenges to be surmounted, there are vast possibilities for quantum computing:

- **Drug Discovery**: Quantum computers can analyze and compare molecular structures quickly. As a result, they hold the potential to significantly hasten the drug discovery process.

- **Cryptography**: The basis of modern cryptography – prime factorization could become more efficient using quantum computers.

- **Weather Forecasting**: Simulating the Earth's climate system is a task well-suited to quantum computers, which may lead to more accurate weather forecasting.

- **Artificial Intelligence**: Quantum computing could accelerate machine learning algorithms, thereby empowering AI's full potential.

Quantum computing symbolizes humanity's drive to push the boundaries of what is possible with technology. It is a field still largely in its infancy, yet its potential to shape our future is profound. As we continue our journey into the quantum age, we stand on the precipice of a computation revolution that could redefine what humanity perceives as achievable.

Chapter 7. Harnessing AI: Key Industries and Applications

Artificial Intelligence (AI) - a concept that once seemed confined to the realms of science fiction, is now a robust reality, significantly transforming numerous sectors. Every industry, from healthcare and finance to transportation and education, has started to realize the immense potential of AI.

7.1. The Fundamentals of AI

Before we delve into specifics, let's first equip ourselves with a basic understanding of AI. Artificial Intelligence refers to machines' capabilities to mimic human intelligence processes and learn from these processes. Machine learning, a subset of AI, provides systems the ability to automatically learn and improve from experience without being explicitly programmed. The ultimate goal of AI is to build systems that can perform tasks that usually need human intelligence, such as image recognition, speech recognition, decision-making, and translation between languages.

7.2. AI in Healthcare

When it comes to healthcare, AI has shown promise in diagnosis, treatment, patient care, and research.

- Diagnosis: AI algorithms are becoming increasingly adept at recognizing patterns in medical imaging, thus aiding in the early identification of diseases such as cancer and neurological disorders.

- Treatment: Applied AI can assist in developing personalized treatment plans. It can analyze a patient's unique genetic makeup, lifestyle, and other factors to create a tailor-made regimen.

- Patient Care: Chatbots and virtual health assistants can address basic medical queries, provide post-operative care instructions, or remind patients about their medication.

- Research: Machine learning models are capable of processing vast amounts of data, which would be infeasible for humans. This capacity lends itself well to medical research, including the development of new drugs or therapies.

7.3. AI in Finance

Artificial Intelligence and the broader field of data science have moved beyond the hype and are redefining the traditionally conservative finance sector.

- Risk Management: Machine learning algorithms are used to detect fraudulent transactions in real-time through pattern recognition. AI's ability to automate risk assessment is making the credit scoring system more reliable.

- Trading: AI-powered predictive models are being used to analyze market trends and make stock predictions based on historical data.

- Customer Service: Many financial institutions are implementing AI-powered chatbots and virtual assistants that can respond to customers' queries and handle tasks such as account management and bill payment.

7.4. AI in Transportation

The transportation industry is another area where AI is having a profound impact.

- Autonomous Vehicles: AI technologies, including machine

learning and computer vision, are the key drivers behind autonomous vehicles. They enable vehicles to recognize traffic signs and pedestrians, predict the behavior of other drivers, and navigate complex environments.

- Route Optimization: AI systems can optimize routes in real-time, predicting and avoiding traffic congestion. This results in time savings for passengers and increases efficiency for logistics and delivery companies.

- Predictive Maintenance: AI is used to predict potential vehicle faults before they cause disruption. This helps to decrease downtime and maintenance costs, providing better reliability.

7.5. AI in Education

From personalized learning to automating administrative tasks, AI is reshaping the education sector.

- Personalized Learning: AI can personalize the learning experience for students by analyzing performance and learning patterns. It can then adjust the curriculum to suit individual learning strengths and weaknesses.

- Automating Administrative Tasks: AI can help automate administrative tasks for teachers, such as grading and scheduling, allowing them to spend more time on crucial tasks like student interaction.

- Intelligent Tutoring: AI-powered tutoring systems can provide on-demand help to students, offering explanations, feedback, and work-throughs to help them understand a concept.

In conclusion, artificial intelligence is not only transforming the business landscape of these key industries but also revolutionizing the way we live, work, and solve problems. The potential implications are immense, and as AI continues to develop and mature, we can anticipate it reshaping an endlessly expanding range of activities and processes across all sectors of society. Therefore, a thorough understanding of AI, its applications, and its impacts is critically important in our increasingly digitized world.

Chapter 8. Leveraging Quantum Computing in Everyday Life

While Quantum Computing (QC) may sound like a realm of technology that's distantly removed from our everyday lives, you may be surprised to know that it has the potential to deeply integrate into the fabric of our daily existence. From enhancing data security to revolutionizing aspects of healthcare, QC can substantially alter the foreseeable future.

8.1. How Does Quantum Computing Work?

To grasp how quantum computing might fit into our everyday lives, it's helpful to understand its basics first. While traditional computing operates in a binary framework of ones and zeros, known as bits, quantum computing uses quantum bits, or qubits. Unlike classical bits, which are either on or off, qubits can exist in superposition - they can be on, off, or both.

The primary power of a quantum computer comes from this ability to store and process a vast amount of information simultaneously. Imagine reading several books at once rather than one after the other. That's precisely how quantum computers streamline operations, paving the way for accelerating several aspects of our lives.

8.2. Quantum Computing and Healthcare

One of the most promising applications of quantum computing lies in healthcare. QC can revolutionize disease detection, drug discovery, and genomics, propelling the industry into a new era of personalized medicine.

Currently, drug discovery is a cost-intensive and time-consuming process, taking years or even decades. Quantum computers, with their ability to process complex information at unprecedented speeds, can vastly accelerate this procedure. Examining molecular structures and running simulated interactions between numerous molecules can be performed by quantum computers at a rate unachievable by classical computing. This could enable pharmaceutical companies to create targeted drugs faster and more cost-effectively, bringing clinical trials to patients sooner than ever expected.

Meanwhile, in the genomics space, quantum computing can decode DNA sequences more efficiently and accurately. This could help identify genetic predictors for diseases much quicker, thereby prompting early interventions.

8.3. Quantum Computing in Financial Services

The financial sector, driven by large-scale computations, could greatly benefit from quantum computing. Portfolio optimization, risk analysis, pricing derivatives, or fraud detection relies heavily on processing large data volumes, which quantum computers are primed to do.

In portfolio optimization, for example, an investor wants to maximize returns and minimize risk. To achieve this balance, they have to consider millions of potential combinations and contingents. With a quantum advantage, this tedious task could be performed in a fraction of the time.

Similarly, risk analysis involves processing large data sets to identify potential financial vulnerabilities. The computational might of quantum machines would enable real-time risk assessment, making financial systems more robust and secure.

8.4. Boosting Cybersecurity with Quantum Computing

While the Internet has been a game changer for humanity, it has also been a hunting ground for cybercriminals. Quantum computing could be our shot at winning the fight against cyber threats.

Quantum encryption or quantum cryptography utilizes the principles of quantum mechanics to encrypt data and transmit it in a way that any interception or intrusion can be detected. Fundamentally, this cryptography relies on the principle that observing a quantum system can change its state. Therefore, any eavesdropping would be noticeable, making data transfer secure like never before.

8.5. Quantum Computing in Weather Forecasting and Climate Modeling

As climate change becomes an urgent concern globally, accurate environmental forecasting and climate modeling have become paramount. Quantum computers, with their superior computational capabilities, can process complex climate simulations and predict weather patterns accurately and quickly.

Given the vast permutations involved in predicting weather patterns, traditional computers struggle with this task. However, quantum computers, with their ability to process various probabilities simultaneously, might offer a definitive edge when it comes to weather forecasting.

8.6. Quantum Computing and Everyday Tech

Beyond these domain-specific applications, quantum computing stands to make everyday tech more powerful and efficient. Graphical rendering, faster databases, and optimized logistics are all valid future outcomes. Think of personalized shopping recommendations that are spot-on, real-time traffic routing, or even game playing - the everyday impact of quantum computing can be limitless.

These are just the tip of the iceberg when it comes to integrating quantum computing into our daily lives. QC promises to be an exciting and transformative journey. However, there are challenges to widespread quantum computing implementation, including the need for extremely low operating temperatures and stabilizing the qubits. Advancements in technology and continued research are addressing these challenges head-on, and in time, quantum computing might become as commonplace as our smartphones.

Remember, once upon a time, the idea of sending an email, streaming movies, or navigating with GPS seemed fantastical, yet today, these are integral parts of our lives. In a similar vein, let's watch as quantum computing unfurls into our day-to-day lives, making the extraordinary possible.

Chapter 9. Challenges and Ethical Considerations of AI

1. Introduction to AI Ethics and Challenges

Artificial Intelligence (AI) is a technological breakthrough advancing at an unprecedented rate. In its stride, though, AI carries along a plethora of ethical issues and challenges we need to address. It's like a double-edged sword – enhancing efficiency, accuracy, and productivity on one side, posing potential threats to privacy, bias, and job displacement on the other.

9.1. AI Ethics: A Multifaceted Concern

At the heart of AI Ethics lie diverse concerns rooted in several domains: philosophical, societal, and technological. It circles fundamental questions about personhood, consciousness, rights and responsibilities, and extends to widespread issues of transparency, privacy, bias, and social impact.

Beyond philosophical musings, AI Ethics has concrete, practical implications. It plays a crucial role in maintaining and enhancing stakeholder trust, assuring businesses of steady progress and growth in the AI landscape.

9.2. Challenges in Defining AI Ethics

There's a broad spectrum of shared values and cultural norms across the globe. Defining universal AI ethics that reflects these diverse perspectives is challenging. Even though many organizations aim to define the ethical code of AI, the global consensus remains elusive.

1. Major Ethical Challenges in AI

Although the list of ethical issues in AI is long, there are standouts that we must tackle urgently given their widespread implications and potential impact.

9.3. Privacy Concerns

Privacy issues lie at the core of AI's ethical concerns. AI systems collect, analyze, and store a copious amount of personal data to function effectively. Can we fully guarantee that these systems won't misuse data, especially when some organizations use AI to generate detailed personal profiles for targeted advertisements? We also have to consider the potential misuse of AI in surveillance, effectively threatening our fundamental rights to privacy.

9.4. Bias and Discrimination

The biased behavior of AI systems is another grave concern. These systems inherit human biases via their training data, leading to discriminatory outcomes. Be it racial, gender, or any other form of bias, they remarkably affect the decision-making capacity of AI, leading to unfair results in crucial sectors like healthcare, law enforcement, and recruitment.

9.5. Job Displacement

AI, with automation and robotics at its helm, is poised to disrupt the labor market significantly. It might render certain jobs obsolete, leading to mass unemployment. How do we manage this transition whilst ensuring minimal disruption to livelihoods constitutes an integral part of our AI ethics considerations?

1. Mitigating the Ethical Challenges

Addressing the ethical challenges of AI is no easy task. However, numerous steps can be taken towards a more ethical future with AI.

9.6. Privacy Regulations and Legislation

Robust governance mechanisms and regulatory frameworks can mitigate privacy concerns. Laws like the European Union's General Data Protection Regulation (GDPR) are pioneering steps towards regulating data privacy and ensuring companies adhere strictly.

9.7. Developing Fair and Unbiased Algorithms

For reducing biases in AI systems, we should aim to develop fair algorithms and use representative datasets for training. Transparency about the origins of data and the design of AI systems also helps in avoiding potential biases.

9.8. Upskilling and Reskilling Programs

To counter job displacement, organizations and governments must prioritize upskilling and reskilling initiatives. A shift in focus towards lifelong learning will aid in equipping individuals with the skills to adapt to AI professions.

1. The AI Ethics Roadmap

The path to ethical AI is undoubtedly tumultuous but not impossible to navigate. It requires persistent efforts, global collaborations, thorough regulations, and an education system that emphasizes critical thinking and ethical reasoning. With these efforts, we can steer AI developments towards enhancing the greater good rather than exacerbating existing inequalities.

1. Conclusion

Being in the AI era, we can't let the ethical challenges deter us. Instead, they instigate us to ponder, interpret and establish a balance between the transformative capabilities of AI and the ethical principles we so stringently adhere to.

Let us remind ourselves that the goal isn't just to build AI systems that work but to build systems that work for everyone. The ethical considerations, the challenges, and their potential solutions should guide us to create an AI ecosystem that respects privacy, ensures fairness, supports jobs, and, above all, benefits humanity.

As AI races ahead, let's use this momentum to run combined with our moral compass, not against it. In this AI-charged world, let's aspire to build technology that preserves our democratic values and nourishes the essence of our shared humanity.

Chapter 10. Security Concerns and Quantum Computing

As we delve deeper into the realm of Quantum Computing, it becomes vitally important to address a looming challenge this new technology poses - security concerns. The extraordinary processing power of Quantum Computers may threaten to dismantle modern-day security systems. This hardware advancement has the potential to transform encryption practices, which maintain the confidentiality and integrity of our digital transactions and data.

10.1. The Current Security Framework

Let's begin by reflecting on our existing security framework. Present cryptographic algorithms primarily base their security on the assumed mathematical difficulty of certain problems, such as factoring large composite numbers or solving discrete logarithm problems. These algorithms, used widely in secure web browsing, email encryption, VPNs, and blockchain technologies, ensure data protection.

However, these encryption methodologies rely on the premise that classical computers—and by extension, hackers employing these machines—cannot feasibly solve their key algorithms within a reasonable time frame. For instance, RSA-2048, a commonly used encryption algorithm, would take a classical computer several quadrillion years to crack. Hence, our data remains secure.

10.2. Quantum Computing and Encryption

Quantum computers, though, represent a potential paradigm shift. A sufficiently large quantum computer can theoretically solve certain problems exponentially faster than a classical system. This speed offers unprecedented prospects for scientific and technological advancements but also harbors risks.

Shor's algorithm, designed for a quantum computer, can, theoretically, factor large numbers exponentially faster than the most efficient known classical algorithm. This reality is concerning because it uncovers the potential for quantum computers to decrypt classical RSA and ECC cryptographic systems.

10.3. Quantum Threat to Encryption

A significant scenario worth envisioning involves a threat actor storing encrypted data today, only to decrypt them using Quantum Computing in the future. The decryption of sensitive data from the past can have numerous consequences, especially when it houses classified governmental, financial, or personal data.

Therefore, organizations should pay heed to securely convert all valuable long-term information to post-quantum cryptographic algorithms before adversaries gain access to quantum computational abilities. This scenario showcases the urgency for quantum-ready security protocols, even if quantum computers capable of running Shor's algorithm aren't feasible yet.

10.4. The Silver Lining: Quantum Cryptography

Despite the imposing threat quantum computers pose to classical encryption techniques, they also usher in a new era of quantum cryptography. One such application of quantum computing in the realm of security is Quantum Key Distribution (QKD).

QKD utilizes principles of quantum mechanics to enable two partners to exchange a cryptographic key, which they can use to encrypt and decrypt messages. The unique attribute of QKD is an inherent security feature: If any third party attempts to eavesdrop or measure the quantum state of the key, it will irreversibly change, alerting the communicators about a potential intrusion.

10.5. Post-Quantum Cryptography

While QKD provides a prospective solution, it demands extensive resources and sophisticated devices, hence its use is currently limited. To solve this, another field gaining momentum is post-quantum cryptography, aiming to construct cryptographic algorithms secure against both quantum and classical computers.

Post-quantum algorithms do not require a quantum computer for encryption or decryption. They remain secure because these mathematical problems remain difficult for both classical and quantum computers. These encompass lattice-based, code-based, multivariate polynomial, hash-based, or supersingular elliptic curve isogeny cryptography.

10.6. The Path Ahead

There is a consensus amongst cryptographers that now is the right time to standardize and implement quantum-resistant algorithms.

This process, though, carries enormous responsibility and requires extensive testing and vetting for weaknesses. International entities like the National Institute for Standards and Technology (NIST) are already underway identifying and standardizing post-quantum cryptographic algorithms.

To transition into a post-quantum era seamlessly, organizations need to understand their cryptographic landscape, assess the risks quantum computing poses to their operations, and begin updating their systems to integrate quantum-safe algorithms.

In essence, Quantum Computing undoubtedly poses a serious threat to current security norms, disrupting established practices. However, just as it poses a threat, it also paves the way for advanced security in the form of quantum cryptography. As with all cutting-edge advancements, the key lies in our ability to adapt and evolve, ensuring we not only survive the changes but also leverage them for a safer future.

10.7. Conclusion

The duality of quantum computing can be intimidating - an existential threat to our confidential data while offering revolutionary possibilities. The approach, however, should not be driven by fear, but rather by intelligence, preparedness, and a thorough understanding of how to refine our security landscape. The quantum future is coming, and our ability to embrace and adapt will determine the outcome.

Chapter 11. What the Future Holds: AI and Quantum Computing

In our journey so far, we've embarked on an exploration of Artificial Intelligence (AI) and Quantum Computing. Let's now cast our sights forward – toward what the future holds. With their immense potential, these two technologies are rapidly shaping our world, from how we work to how we live.

11.1. AI's Expanding Horizons

AI has far outpaced its early ambitions. Not long ago, tech visionaries were striving for systems that could recognize handwritten digits or navigate a cluttered room – tasks that, today, pose trivial challenges to modern AI. As this technology has advanced, so too have our ambitions.

Future AI systems will likely reach deeper into the spheres of human ability, emulating high-level cognitive processes like logic, strategy, creativity, and even emotion. Accomplishing this will necessitate paradigm-shifting advancements in AI's understanding of context, representation, and reasonableness.

11.1.1. Improved Contextual Understanding

AI has traditionally struggled with understanding the context in which its tasks occur. However, rapid advancements are being made, promising an AI future where systems could exhibit a nuanced understanding of the world around them. This development could dramatically improve the sophistication of AI applications, from personalized digital assistants to advanced recommendation systems.

11.1.2. New Representational Models

AI systems of the future will not only understand context but also express their knowledge in more human-like ways. Current AI models often employ unintuitive methodologies, such as high-dimensional vector spaces, to represent information. Progress in AI research promises a future where this knowledge can be represented in a more explainable and comprehensible manner, facilitating more efficient human-AI collaboration.

11.1.3. Ethical AI and Fairness

The evolution of AI brings forth ethical and moral dilemmas. Efforts are underway to ensure AI's ethical usage, fairness, and transparency. In the future, AI systems will incorporate measures to guarantee the usage of unbiased information sources, create intuitive bias correction mechanisms, and also make AI decision-making processes more transparent and accountable.

11.2. Quantum Computing: A New Era of Computation

Quantum Computing, with its paradigm-shifting computational capabilities, promises several breakthroughs. Here are some ways we can expect Quantum Computing to evolve.

11.2.1. Optimization and Efficiency Improvements

Quantum systems can process multiple possibilities simultaneously, offering tremendous opportunities for optimization. For instance, it can revolutionize logistics, coming up with the most efficient routes for package deliveries far quicker than conventional computers.

11.2.2. Enhanced Machine Learning

Quantum Computing is set to supercharge machine learning algorithms. Quantum-enhanced machine learning can handle significantly larger datasets, leading to more accurate and sophisticated models. This has substantial implications for sectors like healthcare, finance, and climate modeling.

11.2.3. Quantum Internet

Quantum Internet leverages quantum states for communication, potentially creating a communication network that's unhackable due to the principles of quantum physics. While in its nascence, the Quantum Internet could transform how sensitive information is transmitted, thereby redefining global communication and cybersecurity norms.

11.3. The Confluence of AI and Quantum Computing

AI and Quantum Computing, while powerful individually, could be even more transformative when brought together. This convergence is an exciting frontier that could spearhead new revolutions.

11.3.1. Quantum Machine Learning

Quantum Machine Learning (QML) offers a tantalising prospect: the marrying of Quantum Computing's computational prowess with AI's capability for intelligent pattern detection. Future QML may offer exponentially faster processing times, unparalleled optimization capabilities, and the agility to handle complex, high-dimensional scenarios that are prohibitively challenging for classical models.

11.3.2. Accelerating Discovery

In areas like drug discovery, transportation, and renewable energy, the union of AI and Quantum Computing could significantly accelerate the discovery and development processes. This could expedite various socio-economic goals, from mitigating climate change to revolutionizing healthcare.

11.4. Potential Challenges

With the potential prospects, come significant challenges to consider. Future governance and regulation models will need to account for AI's and Quantum Computing's fast-paced developments and ethical implications. Additionally, both technologies require a programmatically adept workforce. Training and upskilling efforts will need to ramp up to leverage these technologies effectively.

As we peer into the future, the course is filled with uncharted territory. AI and Quantum Computing are pushing the frontiers of what's possible, reshaping the conventional paradigms. While the voyage has its share of challenges and uncertainties, the promise of a smarter, connected, and more efficient world is an exciting prospect.

But remember, technology in itself does not define the future – we do. Therefore, as we innovate, it's essential to apply these technologies responsibly and ethically. Our collective future with AI and Quantum Computing depends on us navigating the path with prudence and foresight.

This marks the end of our exploration. While we've told a comprehensive story of AI and Quantum Computing's incredible journey and exciting future, our understanding of these realms will continue to evolve as we witness and participate in their advancement. The future indeed is exciting, and more so because we, as humans, get to shape it.

And as you close this report, remember, this is not just the end, but also the beginning of your journey into these revolutionary spheres.